Dare to Dream

IRISH PEOPLE WHO TOOK ON THE WORLD (AND WON!)

SARAH WEBB

ILLUSTRATED BY GRAHAM CORCORAN

THE O'BRIEN PRESS
DUBLIN

About This Book

Our country is built by dreamers, brave people who dared to dream of a new Ireland – an Ireland that was independent, equal and free.

From Patrick Pearse to Countess Markievicz (who featured in *Blazing a Trail: Irish Women Who Changed the World*), they fought hard to make that dream come true.

In this book, I wanted to shine a light on Irish dreamers from all walks of life: sportspeople, activists, scientists, adventurers, creators, writers and even rock stars! Irish people who have achieved great things, often overcoming great obstacles along the way.

I have included remarkable women like Mary Elmes, who saved hundreds of Jewish children during World War II, at great personal risk; and remarkable men like Jack Kyle, who is one of our greatest ever rugby players, but who also dedicated his life to helping others as a surgeon in Zambia in Africa. Bravery comes in all kinds of shapes and sizes, and what they both did was truly heroic.

It has been a fascinating voyage of discovery, and I do hope you enjoy reading this book as much as I enjoyed researching and writing it. And I hope you are inspired to follow your own dreams!

Also by Sarah Webb from The O'Brien Press:
Emma the Penguin (illustrated by Anne O'Hara)
Sally Go Round the Stars (illustrated by Steve McCarthy)
A Sailor Went to Sea, Sea, Sea (illustrated by Steve McCarthy)
Blazing a Trail (illustrated by Lauren O'Neill)

DEDICATIONS

Sarah: *Dare to Dream* is dedicated to two Michaels – my father, Michael Webb, a brave and kind man who has always supported my dreams; and Michael O'Brien, who championed this book from the start, believed I could do it (in record time!) and cheered me on from the sidelines.

Graham: This book is dedicated to my wonderful wife, Nicole, and to my always supportive parents, Paul and Claire.

CONTENTS

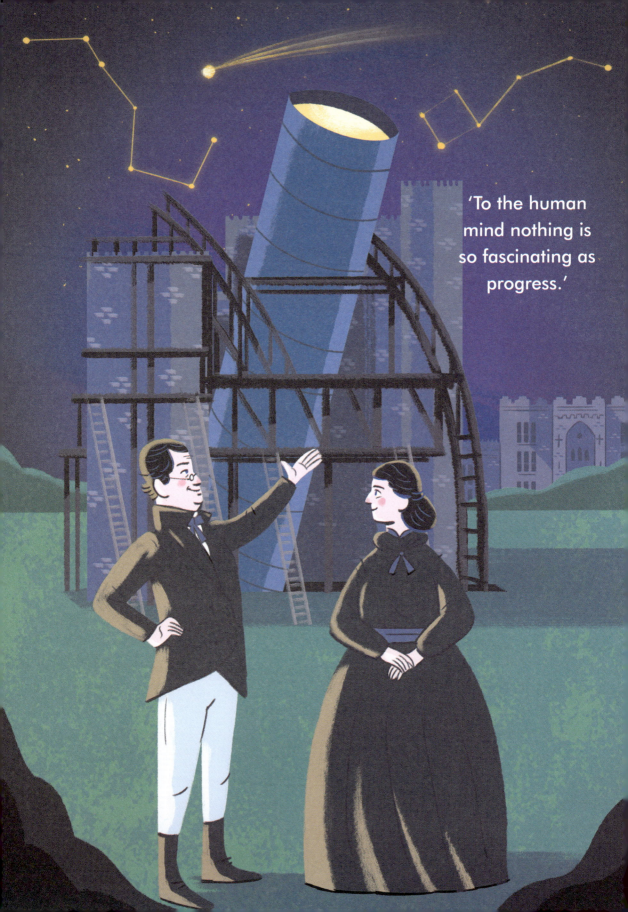

'To the human mind nothing is so fascinating as progress.'

William Parsons

ENGINEER AND ASTRONOMER

1800–1867

As a young man, William read about the 'Great Forty-Foot' telescope, near London. It filled him with wonder, and he dreamed of building his own giant telescope one day.

William Parsons, the 3rd Earl of Rosse, was born in York in England and educated at home in Birr Castle, County Offaly. He studied maths at Trinity College Dublin and at Magdalen College, Oxford. After graduating, he devoted the rest of his life to studying the stars.

To see further into space than ever before, he had to build something extraordinary – the largest Newtonian, or reflecting, telescope in the world. These telescopes work by bouncing light off two mirrors, one of which is shaped like a dish. The larger this dish-shaped mirror, the further you can see.

Luckily, his wife Mary, a wealthy heiress, was also fascinated by science, and supported his experiments. William built a special workshop at Birr to make a huge 1.8-metre concave mirror, which weighed 3.5 tons (the weight of a small car). He made many mistakes – his first mirror cracked as it cooled – but he was a patient and determined man, and he kept going.

In 1845, after two years of intense work, the telescope was ready. Through the lens, William was the first person in the world to see the swirling spiral shape of the M51 nebula.* William's drawings of this created a worldwide sensation. They may have inspired Vincent Van Gogh to paint *The Starry Night*.

Birr telescope was the largest in the world for over seventy years. You can visit it and Mary's darkroom in the grounds of Birr Castle to this day.

A nebula is a giant cloud of dust and gas in space. In William's time, the word was used to describe any objects beyond the Milky Way, including the spiral or 'whirlpool' galaxy that William studied.

Mary Rosse was one of Ireland's first female photographers. Her darkroom at Birr Castle, dating from the 1840s, is one of the oldest surviving in the world. Her early photographs were of William's telescope.

William's son Charles Parsons invented the steam turbine engine in 1884. These were used to power ocean liners like the *Lusitania* and naval ships like the 'dreadnoughts', and to generate electricity.

William's cousin Mary Ward was also an accomplished scientist. She was an expert on microscopes and on the natterjack toad. Sadly, in 1869, she died in one of the world's first motorcar accidents.

George Boole

MATHEMATICIAN

1815–1864

Known as the 'father of modern computing', every piece of electronics in the world, from computers to search engines, works because of George's incredible brain.

George Boole was born in Lincoln, England, the eldest son of a shoemaker and a lady's maid. His father was more interested in science than mending shoes, and the business failed. So George had to leave school at fourteen and become a teacher to help support his family.

But George wasn't going to let this stop him. He dedicated every spare minute to studying his beloved maths and published papers about his work in journals. He also taught himself French, German, Italian, Latin *and* Greek! He was offered a place to study at Cambridge University, but could not afford to attend.

Ten years later, in 1849, Queen's College Cork (now University College Cork) was looking for its first maths professor. Although he had no college degree, George asked some of the top mathematicians to write letters of recommendation. It worked! George moved to Cork and became a much-loved and brilliant teacher.

He came up with an idea that changed the world: Boolean Logic. He devised a maths equation that could represent a logical statement like 'Today is Sunday.' The answer would be yes or no, or, in Boole's maths 'language', 0 or 1.

Eighty years later, a young American graduate student called Claude Shannon used this idea to create a simple circuit. Boole's yes/no logical statements could be translated into an on/off format for electrical circuits. The computer age had begun!

In 2015, 200 years after he was born, University College Cork celebrated George's remarkable achievements.

George's wife, Mary, was a feminist philosopher and educationalist. His daughter Alicia Boole Stott, a maths genius like her father, became an expert in 4-D geometry and was made an honorary Doctor of Mathematics.

Another daughter (there were five in total, and he was a proud father to them all), Lucy Everest Boole, was a gifted chemist and became the first female Professor of Chemistry in Ireland or Britain.

The youngest sister, Ethel Lilian Voynich, wrote a novel called *The Gadfly*, which sold millions of copies in Russia. In 1970, a minor planet was named after her – 2032 Ethel. It joins the moon crater named after her father!

'... those universal laws of thought that are the basis of all reasoning ...'

'I want to enable the ordinary reader to follow … the course of modern astronomy.'

Agnes Mary Clerke

SCIENCE WRITER
1842–1907

As a child, Agnes loved to gaze at the stars and planets through her father's telescope. She dreamed of sharing her passion with others, and through her sharp mind and determination she made it happen!

Agnes was born in Skibbereen in west Cork and was taught at home. Her father was a bank manager with a keen interest in astronomy, and her mother was a gifted musician. Agnes had a huge thirst for knowledge. She was taught maths, science, Latin and Greek, as were her older sister Ellen Mary, who also became a writer, and her younger brother Aubrey.

The family moved to Dublin when Agnes was nineteen. Her brother Aubrey was a student at Trinity College Dublin. Women were not allowed attend the college at the time, but Aubrey shared his maths and science textbooks with Agnes. She also studied Italian and German and was a gifted pianist.

In 1877, Agnes started sending articles to the *Edinburgh Review*. They were so impressed with her writing that they published her. Then she was asked to write biographies of scientists for the *Encyclopedia Britannica*, including an entry about Galileo. She had the great gift of making science accessible to ordinary readers.

In 1885, Agnes's first book was published – *A Popular History of Astronomy during the Nineteenth Century*. It was widely read and became a huge success. She went on to publish many other books about the solar system and was made an honorary member of the Royal Astronomical Society in 1903.

It is thanks to remarkable women like Agnes that attitudes towards women in science and public life started to change. She will always be remembered as a true pioneer, blazing a trail for those coming after her.

Dublin-born Margaret Huggins (1848–1915) and her husband, William, were also pioneers of modern astrophysics. Margaret was a close friend of Agnes's, and was also made an honorary member of the Royal Astronomical Society.

The International Astronomical Union named a moon crater after Agnes – the Clerke Crater, at 22 degrees north, 30 degrees east. The Apollo 17 space shuttle landed near her crater in 1972.

Agnes spent three months at the Cape of Good Hope in South Africa, studying the stars in the southern hemisphere. She was invited to work at the Royal Observatory at Greenwich, London, but chose to continue her research and writing.

Albert DJ Cashier

AMERICAN CIVIL WAR SOLDIER

1843–1915

Jennie dreamed of a life of excitement and adventure, a world beyond the grasp of any poor Irish girl. But for a boy – that was different!

Jennie Irene Hodgers was born in Clogherhead, County Louth. Not much is known about her early life, but it's likely she never went to school, as she couldn't read or write, and lived on a small farm.

In 1862, when she was seventeen, she sailed to America, where she reinvented herself. Jennie lived as Albert DJ Cashier for the rest of her life.

Albert worked on a farm in Illinois for a time and then decided to join Abraham Lincoln's Union Army. Although he was on the small side, he had no problem passing the basic medical test – teeth, hands and feet!

Albert was captured by the Confederate Army, but managed to escape by knocking his guard to the ground and sprinting away. He was known as a brave and loyal soldier, and was much liked by the other men in Company G of the 95th Infantry Regiment, who called him 'Chub'.

After the war, Albert settled in Saunemin, a small village in Illinois. He worked as a lamplighter* and on a farm owned by the Chesbro family.

While being treated in hospital, it was discovered that Albert was physically a woman, and the Army took his veteran's pension away. His army colleagues protested that this was unfair – Albert was a fellow Union soldier, who fought with courage and tenacity. The pension was reinstated.

Albert died in 1915, and was buried in his uniform with full military hours in Sunnyslope Cemetery, Saunemin. A proud soldier to the end.

*Every evening the lamplighter would light the gas street lamps, and then extinguish them at dawn.

Albert was fearless. During one battle, he jumped up onto a fallen tree trunk and shouted at the enemy to show themselves. Another time, he climbed up a tree to replace a Confederate flag with a Union flag.

The Chesbro family built Albert a small wooden one-roomed house on their land in Saunemin, in which he lived for many years. You can visit it to this day.

Lincoln and the northern states of the USA wanted to abolish slavery, but the southern states disagreed. Lincoln's Union Army and the southern Confederate Army fought in the American Civil War. After much bloodshed, the Union Army won.

'Lincoln wanted soldiers, I wanted excitement.'

'We would not give up our own country – Ireland – if we were to get the whole world as an estate, and the Country of the Young along with it.'

Lady Gregory

WRITER AND CO-FOUNDER OF THE ABBEY THEATRE

1852–1932

Lady Gregory had a big dream – she wanted to set up an Irish theatre that showed Irish plays for Irish audiences. And along with her friend, WB Yeats, she did just that!

Isabella Augusta Persse was born in Roxborough House, County Galway. Educated at home, she was a shy girl who loved reading. She also adored her Irish 'nurse' or nanny, Mary Sheridan, who told her Irish folktales and spoke Irish to her.

Augusta, as she was always called, was a practical, caring person, who helped the sick and poor on her estate. There were sixteen children in her family and she was the youngest girl. Her family called her 'plain', and she surprised them by marrying an older man called Sir William Gregory when she was twenty-eight (late at the time), and becoming very rich.

When William died in 1892, Augusta started to write in earnest. She published over forty books and plays during her lifetime, including popular new versions of Irish myths and legends, like *Cuchulain of Muirthemne*.

Augusta and WB Yeats set up the Abbey Theatre in Dublin in 1904, putting on their own works and plays by important Irish writers. Augusta was highly respected, and a little feared, for her strong opinions. She became known in theatre circles as the 'Old Lady'.

Augusta's son Robert was a pilot during World War I and was killed in action. Writing and the theatre became her family, and she put all her passion and energy into them.

She died at home in Coole Park in Galway, surrounded by her beloved books. To this day, the Abbey Theatre remains the National Theatre of Ireland.

Augusta's most popular play was *Spreading the News*, a comedy set in an Irish village. People laughed so much that they couldn't hear some of the play. 'I mustn't be so amusing again!' Augusta joked.

A leading figure in the Irish Literary Revival, Augusta hosted meetings of writers at Coole Park. There is a copper beech tree in the garden known as the 'Autograph Tree', which visiting writers like Yeats carved their names into.

When the Abbey put on *The Playboy of the Western World* by JM Synge, people said it was 'vulgar' or rude, as the play mentions a 'shift' (underwear). There were riots in Dublin, and in New York audiences threw stink bombs and potatoes at the actors.

Douglas Hyde

IRELAND'S FIRST PRESIDENT
1860–1949

Douglas Ross Hyde dreamed of an Ireland that celebrated his own language and culture, and he worked hard all his life to make this happen.

He was born in Longford House, Castlerea, County Roscommon, the son of a Church of Ireland rector. He had three brothers, but was closest to his younger sister Annette.

As a boy, Douglas loved nature and the outdoors and often visited his neighbours to listen to Irish folktales and history. Taught at home by his father, Douglas was naturally brilliant at languages. He was fluent in French, German, Hebrew, Greek and Latin, but his favourite was Irish.

At twenty he went to Trinity College Dublin, to study languages. There he began to write poetry in Irish as 'An Craoihín Aoibhinn' (the sweet little branch). In 1889, he published a collection of folktales and rhymes in Irish.

In 1893, he helped set up the Gaelic League (Conradh na Gaeilge) and became its first president. It was a roaring success, and by 1904, it had over 50,000 members. In 1909, Douglas became the first Professor of Modern Irish at University College Dublin.

Douglas became the first president of Ireland in 1938. As a Protestant in a largely Catholic country, his position signified tolerance and inclusion for all citizens of Ireland, no matter what their religion.

He served as president for seven years and will be remembered as a great Irish patriot who did all he could for our national language and culture. 'This island *is* and will ever remain Gaelic to the core,' he said.

The role of Irish president was created in the 1937 Irish Constitution, which is a legal document that says how Ireland should be run and states the rights of each Irish citizen.

The Gaelic League's aim was to promote the Irish language, games, culture and music. Well-known members included Lady Gregory and Patrick Pearse. It still promotes the Irish language to this day as Conradh na Gaeilge.

There have been nine Irish presidents in total. The first woman to hold the office was Mary Robinson in 1990. She said, 'I want women who have felt themselves outside history to be written back into history.'

'I dream in Irish.'

SEÁN T. O'KELLY

PATRICK HILLERY

ÉAMON DE VALERA

MARY ROBINSON

ERSKINE CHILDERS

MARY MCALEESE

CEARBHALL Ó DÁLAIGH

MICHAEL D. HIGGINS

'Self-government is our right.
A thing born in us at birth; a
thing no more to be doled out
to us or withheld from us by
another people than the right to
life itself – than the right to feel
the sun, or smell the flowers,
or to love our kind.'

Roger Casement

Human Rights Activist and Irish Nationalist
1864–1916

Roger David Casement was born in Sandycove, County Dublin. His parents died when he was young and he was sent to live with relations in County Antrim.

At around fifteen, he started working for a shipping company in Liverpool. He then took a job that was to change his life – working in the Congo in Africa for a rubber company owned by King Leopold II of Belgium.

Local workers from the Congo, even children, were being beaten and used as slaves, and Roger was outraged by this.

In 1892, he started working for the British government. He wrote a report about the rubber workers' horrific treatment, which caused a sensation. King Leopold was forced to hand control of the Congo back to the Belgian government. In 1910, Roger travelled to South America and wrote another report about a rubber company, this time in the Amazon jungle in Peru. He was knighted for his brave work and reluctantly became Sir Roger Casement.

Roger wanted Ireland to be independent. In 1914, he helped the Irish Volunteers to buy 1,500 rifles in Germany and transport them back by yacht to Howth, County Dublin. He also travelled to America and Germany to promote the cause of freedom.

He returned to Ireland in a German submarine, transporting arms for the 1916 Easter Rising. Roger swam to shore on Banna Strand in County Kerry, but was arrested and charged with high treason for betraying Britain. Although he protested that Britain was not his country, he was found guilty and hanged on 3 August 1916.

The sixteenth and last of the 1916 rebels to be executed, Roger will be remembered as a proud Irishman who fought for justice for all.

During World War I, Roger was also involved in efforts in India to win freedom from the British Empire. India finally gained independence in 1947.

Roger asked to be buried in Murlough Bay, County Antrim, a place he loved, but was buried in Pentonville prison in England instead. In 1965, his bones were finally returned to Ireland and buried with full military honours in Glasnevin Cemetery.

Demand for rubber was very high due to the invention of the pneumatic or inflatable tyre in 1887 by John Dunlop, a Scotsman who spent most of his working life in Ireland. He originally invented it to make his son's tricycle ride more smoothly.

Lena Rice

WIMBLEDON WINNER
1866–1907

Helena Bertha Grace Rice, known as 'Lena', was born in a Georgian house near Cashel, County Tipperary. She had seven brothers and sisters, and played tennis on the court in their garden with her big sister Annie.

As teenagers, Lena and Annie joined Cahir Lawn Tennis Club, playing mixed doubles with soldiers stationed nearby. Lena had a great sense of humour and loved playing jokes on her family, but most of all she loved tennis. She had quite a talent for it, with a powerful service and forehand.

Lena entered the Irish Tennis Championships in 1889. She lost the singles final to an Englishwoman called Blanche Hillyard, but won the mixed doubles with Willoughby Hamilton from Kildare. She played her first Wimbledon Championships in the same year, narrowly losing the final, again to Blanche, who said it was the most exciting match she had ever played.

Lena made history at Wimbledon that year when she became the first female official, during the men's singles matches, calling whether the ball was in court or over the line.

In 1890, Lena became Wimbledon Ladies' Singles Champion, beating Mary Jacks 6-4 6-1. During the match, Lena returned a lobbed ball by jumping in the air and smashing it over the net with all her might, inventing the forearm smash! When the audience got over their shock, they gave her a rousing cheer.

After her win, Lena returned to Ireland to look after her sick mother and gave up competitive tennis. The New Inn Tennis Club in Tipperary holds an annual Lena Rice Trophy in her honour.

In 1890, Willoughby Hamilton won the men's singles at Wimbledon, and Frank Stoker (cousin of Bram who wrote *Dracula*) and Joshua Pim won the men's doubles. It was quite a year for the Irish!

Lena won Wimbledon wearing a long skirt with a floral pattern, a long-sleeved shirt, a straw boater hat and leather boots. Imagine running around a court in all that!

Mabel Cahill (1863–1905) from Kilkenny became the first person to win the 'treble' at the US Championships in 1891, winning the ladies' doubles, the mixed doubles and the ladies' singles.

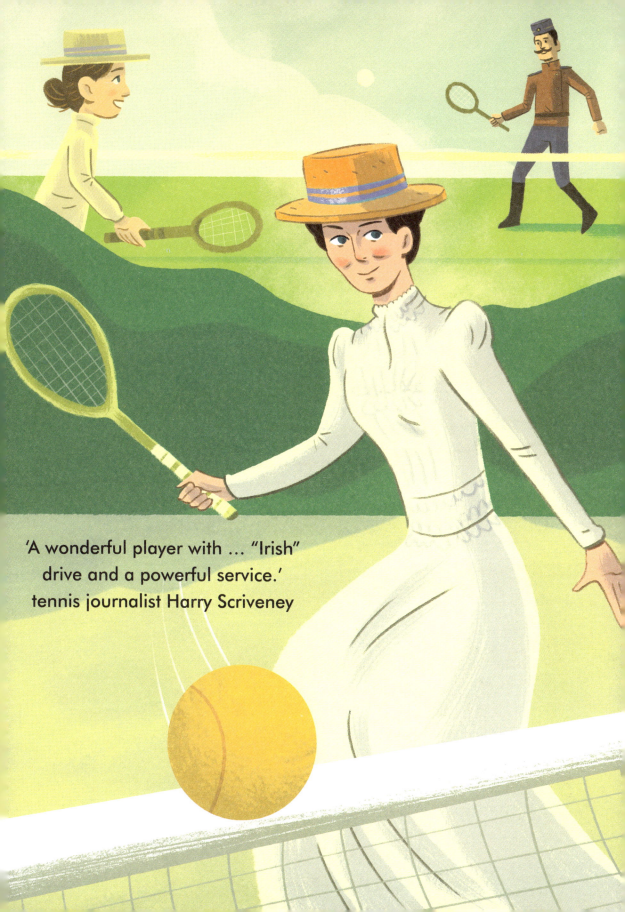

'A wonderful player with … "Irish" drive and a powerful service.'
tennis journalist Harry Scriveney

'... under her boat, darkness
telescopes a world of hover
and float, of swim and flit
and gilled throats ...'
poem 'Maude Enthralled',
Doireann Ní Ghríofa

Maude Delap: 'The Jellyfish Lady'

MARINE BIOLOGIST
1866–1953

Have you ever gazed at jellyfish swimming in the sea and wondered what they eat or how they reproduce? Maude spent a lifetime studying these curious creatures and finding out.

Maude Jane Delap was born in Donegal but moved to Valentia Island, County Kerry, when she was eight. She was one of ten children, and her father was a rector with a keen interest in nature. From a young age Maude shared this passion, searching the island for unusual creatures.

In the 1890s, Maude and her sister Constance (Connie) helped a group of scientists with an important survey of Valentia Harbour. They towed nets behind their small boat to catch sea creatures, from plankton to jellyfish or medusae,* and took the temperature of the sea. When the scientists left, the sisters continued their own research, rowing their boat out together, rain or shine.

Maude was fascinated by jellyfish and was the first person in the world to successfully rear them in captivity. It took great care and hard work, but she was patient and clever. She kept them in huge glass jars, which she shot through with bubbles of oxygen (like a modern aquarium), and worked out exactly how to feed them. She called her jellyfish lab 'the department'.

Scientists had always been puzzled by the complex life cycle of the jellyfish, but it was Maude who finally cracked it! She published her work in 1901 in the *Irish Naturalist* journal. Scientists still use her research to this day.

Maude is buried on Valentia Island beside her sisters, and will always be remembered as a dedicated and brilliant 'citizen scientist'. She has a rare anemone named after her, *Edwardsia delapiae*.

The scientific name for jellyfish, named after the Greek monster who had poisonous snakes instead of hair.

Maude sent her most interesting specimens or 'sea treasures' to the Natural History Museum in Dublin, including a live loggerhead turtle, a squid and a porbeagle shark. She continued doing this until she was 83!

A True's beaked whale washed up on the rocks at Valentia. Maude knew it was an important discovery, and sent its skeleton to the National History Museum. Only six of these rare whales have ever been found.

Irish artist Dorothy Cross created a piece of video art inspired by Maude's work with jellyfish, called *Medusae*. Dorothy's brother, Tom, a science professor, helped her.

Lily and Lolly Yeats

ARTISTS, CRAFTSWOMEN AND PUBLISHERS

1866–1949, 1868–1940

Lily and Lolly Yeats set up and ran their own embroidery and publishing business at a time when women didn't even have the vote!

Susan Mary 'Lily' Yeats was born in Sligo. Elizabeth Corbet 'Lolly' Yeats was born in London. The girls spent most of their childhood in London. Their father was a portrait artist, but was very bad with money, and their mother was ill a lot of the time. One brother, Jack, was a talented artist; the other, Willie, was a gifted poet; but neither earned much money. It fell on the sisters' shoulders to keep the family afloat.

So Lily studied embroidery with a famous designer called William Morris, and Lolly worked as a kindergarten and art teacher. She also published four books about painting and studied printing.

Like many sisters, the girls were very different – Lily was gentle and did not like arguments, Lolly was strong and outspoken – but they rubbed along as best they could and supported each other's work.

They both missed Ireland, and the family returned in 1902. With Evelyn Gleeson, they set up the Dún Emer Guild in Dundrum, County Dublin, producing rugs, embroidery and books.

In 1908, Lily and Lolly founded their own company, Cuala Industries. It employed only women, and used Irish materials. The embroidery was Lily's area and the publishing house, Cuala Press, was Lolly's. As well as keeping food on the family's table, Cuala Industries played an important role in the Gaelic Revival,* producing Irish books and crafts for the people of Ireland.

Lily and Lolly are buried together beside St Nahi's church in Dundrum.

The Gaelic or Celtic Revival was a focus on Irish culture, art and language, which was linked to a new sense of Irish nationalism.

Cuala Press published new work by WB Yeats, Lady Gregory, George Bernard Shaw and Elizabeth Bowen. It was the most important literary publishing house in Ireland at the time and was mainly run by women.

WB (William Butler) Yeats became a world renowned poet and won a Nobel Prize in Literature in 1923. Jack B (John Butler) Yeats' paintings now sell for over €1 million, and feature on gallery walls all over the world.

Lolly was a talented painter and taught art classes in Dublin twice a week for many years. Some of her pupils went on to become well-known artists, such as Mainie Jellett and Anne Yeats (Lolly's niece).

'Cuala Abu!
Gladly we came to our
work every morning,
Daughters of Ireland,
faithful and true.'
Susan Mitchell,
Cuala worker

Inventors and Discoverers

Frank Pantridge
DOCTOR, 1916–2004

Frank began working as a doctor during World War II, spending part of it as a prisoner of war. Later, he invented the portable defibrillator, used to restart the heart after a heart attack. In 1965, the first one in the world was installed in a Belfast ambulance.

Annie Maunder
ASTRONOMER, 1868–1947

Annie discovered that during the 'Little Ice Age' (1645–1715), there was a lack of sunspots on the sun. This became known as the 'Maunder Minimum'. She was one of the first people to find a link between sun spots and the Earth's climate.

John Holland
TEACHER AND ENGINEER
1841–1914

John's childhood dream of travelling underwater became a reality when he invented the first successful submarine. He designed many different versions and suffered many knockbacks (including his debut submarine, the *Holland I*, sinking). His *Holland VI* was bought in 1900 by the US Navy.

James Martin
ENGINEER, 1893–1981

James began building aeroplanes in 1929. When his friend and chief test pilot, Captain Valentine Baker, was killed in a test flight, James wanted to design something to save pilots' lives. His Martin-Baker ejector seat, first produced in 1946, is still used to this day.

Fergal O'Brien
Tissue Engineering Scientist

Fergal has created a new way of getting bone tissue to regrow after an accident or operation. His invention, 'HydroxyColl', is made of a natural material called collagen combined with hydroxyapatite, found in living bones. Placed where bone has been taken out, it encourages new bone to regrow around it.

Margaret Murnane
Physicist

Margaret is a global leader in the area of lasers, working as Distinguished Professor of Physics at the University of Colorado at Boulder. She has designed some of the fastest lasers in the world and created a table-top affordable X-ray laser used by labs and universities around the globe.

Maria McNamara
Palaeobiologist

Maria's research on the evolution of feathers confirmed something remarkable – dinosaurs had feathers! In fact, she found that flying dinosaurs called pterosaurs had at least four different kinds of feathers. She is a world expert on the fossilisation of colour – enabling us to 'see' ancient animals' skins and coats as brightly and vibrantly as they once were.

Valeria Nicolosi
Chemist and Physicist

Valeria was a very curious child, dismantling her family's VCR and toaster! She is now Professor of Nanomaterials and Advanced Microscopy in Trinity College Dublin. She has discovered a new way of increasing the storage capacity of a battery, making it three times more efficient.

Tom Crean

ANTARCTIC EXPLORER

1877–1938

Tom Crean was born on a small farm near Anascaul, County Kerry. He joined the British Navy at fifteen and spent eight years at sea before joining Captain Robert Scott's South Pole expedition.

Their ship *Discovery* reached Antarctica in 1902. Scott and an Irish officer, Ernest Shackleton, set off across the ice, determined to be the first to reach the South Pole. They were unsuccessful.

Tom joined Captain Scott on his next Antarctic expedition, on board the *Terra Nova* in 1901. Again, they were aiming for the South Pole, but so was a Norwegian explorer named Roald Amundsen.

Scott set off with seven men, but he didn't choose Tom for the final part of the journey. Tom was devastated and headed back to base camp with Bill Lashly and Lieutenant Teddy Evans.

It was a gruelling seven-week, 1,200km journey and Teddy, weak with scurvy,* couldn't walk. Tom walked and crawled the final 56km alone to get help.

He was awarded the Albert Medal for bravery. Sadly, Scott and the other men died on the way back across Antarctica, knowing Roald Amundsen had reached the South Pole first.

In 1914, Tom joined Ernest Shackleton's *Endurance* expedition, aiming to be the first to walk across Antarctica. But the ship became trapped in pack ice and was eventually crushed.

The men took to the lifeboats and landed on a rock called Elephant Island. Shackleton, Tom and four others set out to find help, sailing 1,300km across the most dangerous seas in the world and climbing over icy mountains. Remarkably, all twenty-eight men from the *Endurance* survived. And Tom was one of the bravest of them all!

Scurvy is caused by lack of vitamin C and can be fatal.

Tom retired from the navy, married Eileen 'Nell' Herlihy and had three daughters. He opened a pub in Anascaul called the South Pole, which is still there to this day. Mount Crean and the Crean Glacier in the Antarctic are named after him.

Tom was in charge of the dogs on *Endurance*. He built them igloos he called 'Dogloos'. He smuggled a rabbit onto *Terra Nova* – she had 17 babies on Christmas Day! He was known for his cheerful nature, his optimism and his singing (not always good!).

Sir Ernest Shackleton was born in Kilkea, County Kildare, in 1874. He left school at 16 to join the navy. Remembered as one of the world's great explorers, he said, 'The only true failure would be to not explore at all.'

'There is no doubt about it but we saved his life ... my long legs did the trick.'
Tom Crean

'One of my missions in life,
equal rights for men and woman [sic],
was finding me.'

Gretta Cousins

SUFFRAGETTE, TEACHER AND CIVIL RIGHTS CAMPAIGNER
1878–1954

A true civil rights powerhouse, Gretta was imprisoned in three different countries for fighting for what she believed in!

Margaret Elizabeth 'Gretta' Gillespie was born in Boyle, County Roscommon, the eldest of fifteen children. Her father encouraged Gretta to attend political talks as a girl.

After school, Gretta studied music at the Royal Irish Academy in Dublin and became a music teacher. She met a young poet called James Henry Cousins, and they married.

In 1908, James and Gretta set up the Irish Women's Franchise League with Hanna and Francis Sheehy-Skeffington, to campaign for votes for Irish women. Gretta spoke at the first meeting of the organisation. She was a brave, clever and practical woman who always got things done.

Back then, Ireland was ruled by the British parliament. Gretta travelled to London in 1910 with other Irish suffragettes to protest about the lack of votes for women. They broke windows at 10 Downing Street, and Gretta was arrested and sentenced to a month's imprisonment. But it didn't stop her! In 1913, she was imprisoned again, this time for breaking windows at Dublin Castle.

In 1915, Gretta and James moved to India to find work, and both became teachers. Gretta campaigned for votes for Indian women and also for Indian independence from Britain.

When she was fifty-four, Gretta was sentenced to a year in prison for supporting the leader of the Indian independence movement, Mahatma Gandhi. She taught the other prisoners civics and singing. After her release, she added prison reform to her list of things to fight for!

India finally gained independence in 1947, and Gretta lived to see it. She died in India, her beloved adopted home, in 1954.

A brilliant organiser, Gretta set up the Women's Indian Association and the All-India Women's Conference (still successfully running to this day), giving women from all over India a voice. She also ran an All-Asia Women's Conference in 1931.

Gretta gave lectures about India and women's rights all over the world. She was a member of the Women's Committee of the League of Nations and, in 1922, became the first woman Honorary Bench Magistrate, or judge, in India.

A devoted couple, Gretta and James wrote a 'duography' or joint biography about their lives and adventures. It was called *We Two Together*. Gretta also wrote three books about Indian women's rights.

Patrick Pearse

Teacher and Revolutionary

1879–1916

Patrick Henry Pearse was full of hopes and dreams for an independent Ireland.

He was born above his father's stone-carving business on 27 Great Brunswick Street, Dublin, now called Pearse Street. His father was English and his mother was Irish. He felt this mixed background made him 'the strange thing that I am'.

He had two sisters and two half-sisters, but was closest to his brother William. Growing up, his great-aunt Margaret spoke Irish to him and told him stories of Irish mythical heroes like Cúchulainn.

Patrick went to the Christian Brothers School in Westland Row, Dublin, and went on to study modern languages in university.

He wanted to revive the Irish language and give children an Irish education, so in 1908, he set up two largely Irish-speaking schools: Scoil Éanna (St Enda's) for boys and Scoil Íde (St Ita's) for girls. He was a gifted teacher, much loved by his students.

An active member of the Gaelic League* for many years, in 1913, Patrick became an Irish Volunteer, dedicated to fighting for Irish independence from Britain.

Irish republicans were making secret plans for a rebellion, to begin on Easter Sunday 1916. Patrick was the Commander-in-Chief and was chosen as President of the Republic. Around 2,500 Irish rebels faced 17,000 British soldiers. After six days of fighting, the rebels were forced to surrender.

Patrick and his comrades were arrested and imprisoned in Kilmainham Goal. Found guilty of treason, he was shot by firing squad, along with fourteen others, including his brother William.

The Easter Rising changed the course of Irish history, and Patrick was at the heart of that change.

Set up by Douglas Hyde to promote the Irish language and culture.

Patrick wrote and published many plays, poems, short stories and children's books. In 1915, he made a famous speech at the funeral of the Fenian leader Jeremiah O'Donovan Rossa, dedicated to an independent Irish republic.

On Easter Monday of the Rising, Patrick read the Proclamation of the Irish Republic on the steps of the General Post Office (GPO). Largely written by Patrick, it declared Ireland's independence and guaranteed 'equal rights and equal opportunities to all its citizens'.

Scoil Éanna was mainly located in a large house called The Hermitage in Rathfarnham. It is now home to the Pearse Museum, celebrating the life and work of both Pearse brothers. William was a trained artist, and his sculpture is on show here.

Quark SmileSmirk ScribbleDeHobble Tattarrattat Obstropolos Mrkgnao UogiBoGeybo PelootheRep Poppysm

'I always write about Dublin, because if I can get to the heart of Dublin I can get to the heart of all the cities of the world. In the particular is contained the universal.'

James Joyce

WRITER
1882–1941

James Augustine Joyce was born in Rathgar in Dublin, the eldest of ten surviving children. As the family became increasingly poor, they moved from Dublin to the seaside towns of Blackrock and Bray. He called his childhood homes 'those haunted inkpots'.

Life was difficult for James, but he had a thirst for knowledge and buried himself in books. He started writing poetry when he was around nine.

After attending Clongowes Wood College in Kildare and Belvedere College, Dublin, he studied languages at University College Dublin and began to write and publish articles and reviews. He was determined to be a writer.

At age twenty-two, he met a hotel chambermaid from Galway called Nora Barnacle and fell madly in love. James and Nora travelled to Trieste (now in Italy), where James taught English. He wrote a book of short stories called *Dubliners*, but it was very modern and for years no-one was brave enough to publish it.

In James's next book, *A Portrait of the Artist as a Young Man*, he used an unusual way of describing how the main character thought and felt. This was called 'stream of consciousness'.

But his most exciting and ground-breaking novels were yet to come. A literary editor called Harriet Shaw Weaver supported him financially while he worked tirelessly on *Ulysses*, often making himself ill with the effort. It was published in 1922 by Sylvia Beach of the Paris bookshop Shakespeare and Company. It is considered a dazzling piece of modern literature and is read and studied all over the world.

His final novel, *Finnegans Wake*, was published in 1939. James died in Switzerland in 1941, but lives on through his remarkable books.

James was afraid of dogs and thunder for his whole life. There are ten 'Thunderwords' in *Finnegans Wake*, new words created by James. One is made up of lots of words for thunder in different languages.

MoLI, the Museum of Literature, Ireland, has an exhibition dedicated to his work and a display of some of his notebooks. Every year we celebrate James on Bloomsday, 16 June – the date *Ulysses* is set.

Ireland is world famous for its writers and poets. We have four Nobel Laureates in Literature – WB Yeats, GB Shaw, Samuel Beckett and Séamus Heaney. Anne Enright and Anna Burns have both won the Booker Prize.

Elizabeth O'Farrell

NATIONALIST, MIDWIFE AND LOYAL FRIEND
1884–1957

Elizabeth dreamed of an independent Ireland where all people were treated equally, no matter what their gender or background. She worked hard all her life to make this happen.

She was born at 42 City Quay, Dublin, the daughter of a dockworker and a housekeeper. In school at the Sisters of Mercy, she met Julia 'Sheila' Grenan. The girls were very different – Elizabeth was quiet and Sheila was outgoing – but they became devoted friends for life.

Together they joined the Gaelic League and became fluent Irish speakers. In 1906, they joined Inghinidhe na hÉireann (Daughters of Ireland) and also Cumann na mBan (the women's republican organisation). Elizabeth and Julia trained in combat, dispatches (delivering messages and orders) and first aid.

During the Easter Rising of 1916, Elizabeth and Sheila moved between the GPO and the rebel garrisons around the city, transporting messages, food and supplies.

On the last day of the Rising, Elizabeth, Sheila and Winifred Carney were the three remaining women in the GPO. Patrick Pearse and the other rebel leaders knew defeat was close. Elizabeth was chosen to give their offer of surrender to the officer in charge of the British forces, Brigadier General Lowe.

She travelled to the different rebel garrisons, giving them the order to surrender. It was a dangerous mission – as she approached Boland's Mills, a man was shot beside her, but she continued, determined to complete her job.

After the Rising, Elizabeth trained as a midwife and Sheila worked as a dressmaker, and they shared a house. They are buried side by side in the Republican plot in Glasnevin Cemetery. Together forever.

There is a famous photograph of Elizabeth standing beside Patrick Pearse as Lowe accepts Pearse's surrender. Only Elizabeth's feet can be seen – her body and head are behind Pearse. Newspapers printed the picture with her feet airbrushed out.	The National Maternity Hospital at Holles Street gives an annual Elizabeth O'Farrell Award to the best student midwife. There is also a plaque at the hospital marking her years of service there.	The City Quay Park was renamed the Elizabeth O'Farrell Park in her honour in 2012. There is also a building named after her on North Cumberland Street. It is covered in flying metal doves, representing peace.

'It was very dangerous ... bullets raining from all quarters.'

Rex Ingram

MOVIE DIRECTOR, PRODUCER AND WRITER
1893–1950

Have you ever dreamed of being the toast of Hollywood? At the age of twenty-seven, Rex Ingram was described as 'the world's greatest director'!

Reginald Ingram Montgomery Hitchcock, known as Rex, was born in Rathmines in Dublin. His mother loved art and music, and his father was a Church of Ireland rector.

Rex was a boarder at St Columba's College in Dublin. He was very bright, and loved art and boxing, but hated being told what to do and was often in trouble at school.

In 1908, his beloved mother died (he later changed his surname to Ingram which was her maiden name) and, after failing his college entry exams, he decided to leave Ireland for New York.

Here he studied sculpture at Yale, before finding a job in a silent movie* studio. Handsome, hard-working and charismatic, Rex was born for the movies. He did all kinds of jobs – sourcing props, painting scenery, acting, writing and, finally, directing.

The first silent movie he directed was *The Great Problem* in 1916. *The Four Horsemen of the Apocalypse* (1921) was his most successful silent movie, making over $4 million, a huge amount at the time.

He went on to make twenty-seven movies in total (the last one a 'talkie' or talking picture). He also set up his own movie studio in the south of France and wrote several novels.

Rex has a star on the Hollywood Walk of Fame.

* Movies back then had no sound. Words would come up on the screen to explain what was happening – like modern subtitles – and a pianist or a whole orchestra would play along to the action. The first 'talkie' was The Jazz Singer *in 1927.*

Rex had a reputation for being a perfectionist. For one of his films, set in the north African desert, he brought in hundreds of camels to make it look authentic. The actors didn't like the camels, as the camels kept spitting at them!

Rex was world famous in his day and is mentioned in James Joyce's novel *Finnegans Wake* as 'Rex Ingram, pageant-master'. He also appears as a fictional character in F Scott Fitzgerald's work.

Irish actors who have thrived in Hollywood since Rex's day include: Maureen O'Hara, Colin Farrell, Daniel Day Lewis and Saoirse Ronan. Irish Hollywood directors include Jim Sheridan (*My Left Foot*) and Nora Twomey of Cartoon Saloon (*The Breadwinner*).

Rosanna 'Rosie' Hackett

Trade Unionist and Nationalist

1893–1976

Rosie Hackett dreamed of an Ireland that was equal and fair for all. Less than five feet tall, she was a fighter, with a huge heart!

Rosanna 'Rosie' Hackett was born in north inner city Dublin. When she was one, her father died. The family moved to a tenement near the Rotunda Hospital, where five families shared one building.

As soon as Rosie was old enough, she went to work, first in a paper store and then at Jacob's biscuit factory.

In 1910, Rosie joined Jim Larkin's Irish Transport and General Workers' Union (ITGWU). She also became a founding member of the Irish Women Workers' Union, set up by Delia Larkin.

In 1913, Jacob's and other businesses refused to recognise the ITGWU and locked its members out of work. This was known as the 'Dublin Lockout'. The members, including Rosie, refused to back down.

After the Lockout, Rosie lost her job for being 'disruptive' and started working in a shirt factory. She also joined the Irish Citizen Army and helped at a shop where nationalist papers were sold.

On Easter Sunday 1916, Rosie spent the night delivering drafts of the Proclamation of the Irish Republic from the printing works in Liberty Hall to James Connolly's office. The following day, during the Rising, she gave first aid to the injured at the College of Surgeons.

After their surrender, Rosie and the other rebels were imprisoned in Kilmainham Goal. She was released after ten days.

In 1919, Rosie became the Irish Women Workers' Union clerk, and then an ITGWU official. She died in 1976 and was buried in Glasnevin Cemetery with full military honours.

In 1970, Rosie was awarded a gold medal for her 50 years devoted to the trade union movement. In 2013, a new bridge over the River Liffey was named in Rosie's honour. It was the first Liffey bridge to be named after a woman.

Other Irish women involved in the trade union movement included Louie Bennett, who fought successfully for two weeks' paid holidays for women laundry workers in 1945; and Helena Maloney, who was also an Abbey Theatre actor.

A year after Connolly's execution, Rosie and three other women hung a banner from Liberty Hall saying 'James Connolly Murdered 12th May 1916' and barricaded themselves inside so it could not be taken down. Connolly was one of the Easter Rising leaders and a staunch feminist.

'I have always
seen both sides of
every argument
in science.'

Cynthia Evelyn Longfield: 'Madam Dragonfly'

DRAGONFLY EXPERT AND ADVENTURER
1896–1991

Ever dreamed of exploring the world and discovering new species? That's what 'Madam Dragonfly' did!

Cynthia Evelyn Longfield was born in London and grew up in Cloyne, County Cork, on her family's estate, Castle Mary. As a girl she loved spending her time outside, watching caterpillars and tadpoles grow and change.

She was a practical and capable girl and at eighteen, during World War I, she joined the Royal Army Service Corps as a driver. She also worked in an aeroplane factory, where she learned carpentry. During World War II, she ran a fire station.

She went on her first overseas field trip in 1921 – to study insects in South America. She was completely bitten by the exploration bug!

In 1924, she travelled to the Pacific islands on an eighteen-month, 300,000-mile trip, retracing Charles Darwin's expedition on the *Beagle*. Darwin is famous for his work on the theory of evolution. Cynthia's sailing experience came in handy when they hit storms near Panama.

Cynthia was adventurous and fearless. Over her long career as an entomologist,* she travelled (sometimes alone) to southeast Asia, Egypt, Canada and across Africa. She went by boat, rail, road, dirt track, canoe, on horseback and by foot, hacking her way through jungles with a machete!

Although she never went to university, Cynthia became an international expert on dragonflies, wrote many important books and became known as 'Madam Dragonfly'. She continued studying insects until her death at the age of ninety-four and is buried in Cloyne.

The study of insects is called entomology. If you study insects you are an entomologist.

A keen Girl Guide, Cynthia's mapping, camping and survival skills proved brilliant training for her future. On her expeditions she slept in hammocks and was nibbled by many of her beloved bugs, but it never put her off!

Cynthia worked on the Irish national insect collection, capturing and identifying new species and recording them. Some of her insect specimens are on display in the National History Museum in Dublin to this day.

Dragonflies are an ancient group of insects, over 200 million years old. There are 5,000 species of dragonflies in the world, and several are named in Cynthia's honour, including the *Corphaeschna longfieldae*.

Ernest Walton

NOBEL PRIZE-WINNING SCIENTIST

1903–1995

Would you like to make a ground-breaking scientific discovery? Ernest Walton did just that!

Ernest Thomas Sinton Walton was born in Dungarvan, County Waterford. His father was a Methodist minister and his mother was a Quaker. Sadly, she died when he was a young child.

He was a gifted student and, after school in Banbridge, Cookstown, Dublin and Belfast, won a scholarship to Trinity College Dublin. He graduated with the highest degree (a double first) in maths and science.

Ernest then studied for his doctorate at Cavendish Laboratory in Cambridge. He focused on generating high voltages in electricity.

The next big challenge in science was to try and split the atom.* To do this, an apparatus had to be built that could produce particles with enough energy to penetrate an atom's nucleus. Ernest was just the man to build such a thing – practical, hard-working and brilliant!

His supervisor was another Ernest, Ernest Rutherford. He put him together with Jason Cockcroft to work on this important project.

On 14 April 1932, Ernest ran his apparatus. To his shock, 'When I looked in through the microscope I could see a whole lot of little stars suddenly appearing.' Those 'stars' were particles of atoms. He had done it!

Laboratories all over the world wanted him to work with them. But in 1934, he returned to Ireland and married his childhood sweetheart, Freda. He became a science lecturer at Trinity College and spent the rest of his life happily training future scientists.

In fact, they split the atomic nucleus, the tiny centre of an atom. The size of a nucleus in an atom has been compared to 'a fly in a cathedral'.

Ernest was awarded a Nobel Award in 1951 for his pioneering work, along with Jason Cockcroft. It was Ireland's first Nobel Prize for Science.

A life-long pacifist, Ernest was an active member of Pugwash, an Irish anti-nuclear weapons organisation. Asked to participate in war work during World War II, he said, 'My duty is to remain in Ireland to help.'

Ernest met his wife Freda at school in Belfast. She was head girl and he was head boy! They met again as adults on the train platform of the Belfast–Dublin train and spent the rest of their lives together.

'To my delight, I saw tiny flashes of light looking just like the scintillations produced by α-particles.'

'I didn't just give orders. I did things myself. I got things done.'

Mary Elmes

Aid Worker and Humanitarian

1908–2002

Children in the refugee camps called her 'Miss Mary'. She saved hundreds of Jewish children during World War II. But who was this brave Irish woman?

Mary Elizabeth Jean Elmes was born in Ballintemple, County Cork. Her mother fought for votes for women, and her father was a pharmacist.

When she was seven, the passenger ship *Lusitania* was bombed and sank off the coast of Cork, killing 1,198 people. Mary's family rushed to help the injured who were brought ashore. She never forgot what she saw that day.

Mary was a gifted student, graduating with a gold medal in Modern Languages from Trinity College Dublin. She won a scholarship to continue studying, but there was a civil war in Spain,* and she decided to travel there to help in the refugee camps.

After Franco's victory, Spanish people poured over the French border, looking for safety. Mary, a strong, capable woman, was put in charge of a refugee camp. When France surrendered to Germany in 1940, during World War II, French refugees fleeing Hitler's troops also ended up in the camps.

In 1942, legislation was brought in to exterminate the Jewish people (Hitler's Final Solution). Mary's camp now became a Jewish holding camp, from where Jews were sent to Auschwitz concentration camp to be killed.

Mary bravely smuggled children out in the boot of her car, driving them to safe houses. It's estimated that she saved as many as 427 Jewish children.

After the war, Mary married a Frenchman called Roger Danjou, and they had two children. She lived until she was ninety-three and rarely spoke about her remarkable past.

During the Spanish Civil War, the Republicans were fighting a fascist dictator called Franco.

In 1943, Mary was accused of 'hostile acts' against Germany and was locked up in a military prison. When she was released she went straight back to the camp to save more children!

Asked about her time in prison, Mary said, 'Oh, we all had to suffer some inconveniences in those days.' She kept her brown felt prison blanket all her life. 'It was cold in prison,' she said. 'That blanket saved my life.'

One of the children she saved, René Freund, recommended her for the Righteous Among the Nations Award, given to people who helped save Jewish people during World War II. Mary is the only Irish person to hold this honour.

Jack Kyle

SURGEON AND RUGBY LEGEND

1926–2014

Jack Wilson Kyle was born in Belfast and grew up with a brother and three sisters. At school he loved sport but never dreamed that one day he'd play rugby for Ireland.

Jack found passing exams hard. He had to repeat physics and Latin before being accepted to study medicine at Queen's University Belfast.

While at Queen's, his rugby career took off – chosen to play out-half for Ulster at nineteen, he was then selected for Ireland and for the Lions. In total he won forty-six caps for Ireland, including their first Grand Slam* in 1948.

In 1950, Jack went on a six-month tour with the Lions – the journey to New Zealand by boat took four weeks. Jack was named one of the top players in the world that year.

Although he loved rugby, medicine was Jack's first love. After graduating, he devoted the rest of his life to helping people. He felt his surgical skills could be most useful in developing countries, so he went to work in Indonesia before moving to a mining town in Zambia called Chingola.

When Jack separated from his wife, his children, Justine and Caleb, lived with him. Justine wrote a book about him called *Conversations with My Father*. She said: 'If decency were measured in stars then, to me, [Dad] is a galaxy.'

Jack only retired from surgery when he was seventy-four! He will be remembered as one of the greatest ever Irish rugby players, a talented surgeon and a devoted father.

The Grand Slam means you won all your matches in the Five Nations Championship (rugby matches between Ireland, England, Scotland, Wales and France).

Sporting talent ran in the Kyle family. Jack's sister Betty was a gifted hockey player. She was captain of the Irish women's hockey team that won the Hockey Triple Crown in 1950.	Poetry was one of the great pleasures of Jack's life, and his favourite poet was WB Yeats. He knew dozens of poems by heart and loved reciting them.	There is a famous picture of Jack congratulating Ireland captain Brian O'Driscoll after Ireland won the Grand Slam for the second time, in 2009. After Jack's death, fellow out-half Ronan O'Gara described him as 'a thorough gentleman'.

'If you want to be good at something, you have to persevere, no matter what.'

'I knew ... that I wanted to be a great athlete and no one, and no circumstance was going to deter me.'

Ronnie Delany

OLYMPIC CHAMPION
1935

Have you ever dreamed of being one of the fastest runners in the world? Young Ronnie Delany did! And he worked tirelessly to make it happen.

Ronald Michael Delany was born in Arklow, County Wicklow, and moved to Sandymount in Dublin at around five years old. His father was a customs officer.

At school, Ronnie's potential as a runner was spotted by athletics coach Jack Sweeney, who was also his maths teacher. It was Jack who first told Ronnie to make one 'decisive move' during a race.

Ronnie joined Crusaders Athletics Club and began to win races. After leaving school, he was determined to focus on becoming the greatest athlete he could be. He trained hard every day.

All the training paid off when Ronnie set a new Irish record for 880 yards (half a mile) of 1 minute 54.7 seconds. He was offered an athletics scholarship to Villanova University in Philadelphia, where he also studied for a degree in science and economics.

In June 1956, Ronnie became the seventh person in the world, and the youngest ever (he was twenty-one), to run a mile in less than four minutes!

In the same year, he represented Ireland at the Olympics in Melbourne, Australia, in the 1,500 metres. He made his 'decisive move' near the end of the race, passing everyone out with an electrifying sprint. He won a gold medal for Ireland! This is the only track gold medal Ireland has won to date.

Ronnie won many more races, including thirty-four indoor mile events. He was undefeated in indoor events in the US for five years. After a highly successful career as a runner and then a businessman, Ronnie continues to promote his beloved running and sport in Ireland to this day!

In 1924, Larry Stanley was the first Olympian for the newly independent Ireland, in the high jump. The first woman to compete for Ireland was Maeve Kyle, in 1956 (100 and 200 metres).

Roger Bannister was the first person to run a sub-four-minute mile, in 1954. After Ronnie's Olympic victory in Melbourne, Roger said, 'I never saw a more beautifully judged race.' Ronnie's race is still considered one of the greatest in history.

At Villanova University, Ronnie trained with legendary coach Jumbo Elliot, who told him to 'eat, sleep and drink the mile'. Fellow Irish runners Sonia O'Sullivan, Marcus O'Sullivan and Eamonn Coghlan also went to Villanova.

John Hume

POLITICIAN AND CIVIL RIGHTS CAMPAIGNER

1937

Born in Derry, John worked tirelessly to realise his dream of equality and peace in Northern Ireland.

Awarded a school and later a university scholarship, John studied to be a priest before switching to French and history. After graduating, he wanted to 'give something back to the community', so he became a teacher.

There was huge inequality across Northern Ireland at the time for Catholics. Determined to change this, John helped set up a credit union and a housing association in Derry for Catholic families. He helped organise civil rights marches and campaigned for a fair voting system. His slogan was 'one man, one vote'.

In 1970, John became Deputy Leader of a new political party, the Social Democratic Labour Party (SDLP). A gifted speaker and much-loved leader, he was elected to the European Parliament in 1979.

During the 'Troubles' in Northern Ireland, around 3,500 people were killed and 25,000 injured. John believed the only way to achieve lasting peace was to get everyone talking together – nationalists, unionists and the governments of the north, the south and Britain.

In the 1980s and 90s, John met Sinn Féin leader Gerry Adams for secret peace talks. This was dangerous for both of them, but they persevered.

Finally, in 1998, a peace agreement called the Good Friday Agreement* was signed and the people of Ireland, north and south, were asked to vote on it. They voted yes.

John is regarded as one of Ireland's most visionary politicians.

*Signed by the Irish and British governments, and most political parties in Northern Ireland, this is also known as the 'Belfast Agreement'. It explains how Northern Ireland should be governed.

John built close links with American politicians including Senator Edward Kennedy and President Bill Clinton, encouraging them to support the peace process. Clinton said, 'We all owe John a debt of gratitude.'

In 1998, John was awarded the Nobel Peace Prize, along with David Trimble of the Ulster Unionist Party, for their role in negotiating the Good Friday Agreement.

John was also awarded the Gandhi Peace Prize and the Martin Luther King Award. He is the only person to have received all three awards.

'The answer to difference is to respect it. Therein lies a most fundamental principle of peace – respect for diversity.'

'I believe that people should not try to model themselves on someone else. Be your own person.'

Professor Susan McKenna-Lawlor

Astrophysicist

Awarded a Doctorate in Space Physics in 1976

Susan Mary Patricia McKenna was born in Dublin. As a girl she loved reading and dreamed of travelling the world. Now she travels the globe, giving talks and working with other scientists.

Susan didn't learn much about science at school – it wasn't offered as a subject – but she decided she would like to learn something new and opted to study science at the National University of Ireland in Dublin. She found it difficult at first, but once she started to see the beauty, magic and excitement science offered she never looked back!

After studies in Ireland and Michigan, she was awarded a doctorate in Space Physics by the National University of Ireland in 1976. So she is officially a Space Doctor! She is also Emeritus Professor at NUI Maynooth.

As a student she saw the Russian Sputnik 1, the first artificial satellite, fly overhead and later, at a conference in Moscow, she met the professor who had mounted the famous bleeper on board. Soon she was designing her own space experiments.

The first of these was called EPONA. It flew on the European Space Agency's Giotto mission, through the head of Halley's Comet, collecting pioneering data.

In 1985, Susan set up Space Technology Ireland Limited, building instruments for space missions. Susan and her company have designed instruments and experiments for space agencies all over the world, including NASA and the Indian Space Agency.

Susan was elected to the International Academy of Astronautics, one of the highest honours for a space scientist. She continues to reach for the stars to this day!

When she was a girl, Susan always remembers her father scooping up a handful of soil and remarking 'it was so full of wonder you could study it all your life and never come to the end of the interesting things it had to teach you'.

Susan helped to develop an instrument for the Mars Express mission launched by the European Space Agency (ESA) to monitor the solar wind and to collect information about the mystery of water on Mars.

Another of Susan's instruments – an all-sky camera for particles – is presently flying aboard the BepiColombo spacecraft, which was jointly launched by the ESA and the Japanese Space Agency in 2018, bound for planet Mercury.

Bob Geldof

MUSICIAN AND HUMANITARIAN

1954

In 1985, a huge concert called Live Aid was beamed into billions of homes all over the world. It remains the biggest concert ever staged, raising over £150 million for famine relief in Ethiopia. It was dreamed up by an Irish musician called Bob Geldof.

Robert Frederick Zenon Geldof was born in Dublin. Life wasn't easy for Bob – his mother died when he was very young, he found school boring and he was often in trouble.

After school, he moved to England and found a job in a pea-canning factory, before moving to Canada and working as a music journalist.

When Bob returned from Canada, he joined his friends as the lead singer of a band called The Boomtown Rats. They became big stars and had many global hits, including 'I Don't Like Mondays'.

In 1984, Bob was watching the news when images of the famine in Ethiopia came on. He was shocked and decided he had to do something to help. Along with fellow musician Midge Ure, he organised a charity record called 'Band Aid'. Their single 'Do They Know It's Christmas?' raised over £5 million.

Bob flew to Ethiopia in 1985 to see how the 'Band Aid' money should be used, and vowed to do even more to help. He came up with an ambitious plan: ten concerts in ten different countries, broadcast live on television in over 150 countries around the world. Live Aid was a resounding success.

Bob still fights to help Africa to this day – he is one of ten experts on the African Progress Panel and also helps Bono's ONE campaign, which fights extreme poverty, especially in Africa.

As a teenager, Bob spent two nights a week helping homeless people with the Simon Community. From a young age, he hated injustice and realised how unequal the world could be.

During Live Aid, Ireland donated more money per person than any other country, over £5 million. Acts who played at Live Aid included U2, Queen, Madonna and, of course, The Boomtown Rats.

Bob was scruffy and swore a lot, but he made things happen. After Live Aid, people used to stuff money into his pockets in the streets, and he made sure that every penny went to famine relief.

'Music is something I must do,
business is something I need to do,
Africa is something I have to do.'

'When you're sixteen, you think you can take on the world. And sometimes you're right.' Bono

U2

MUSICIANS

1960s

Four teenagers from Dublin became one of the biggest rock bands in the world. It started with a handwritten note on Mount Temple school's bulletin board that read: 'Drummer seeks musicians to form band.'

Laurence Mullen was fourteen when he posted this in 1976. The auditions were held in the kitchen of his parents' house in Artane, north Dublin.

Four boys from his school answered his call: Adam Clayton, David Evans (The Edge), his brother Dik Evans (who later left the band) and Paul Hewson (Bono). Larry said, 'Bono walked in and blew any chance I had of being in control.'

The band members had very different personalities, but they all passionately loved music. They first called the band Feedback, and then The Hype, before settling on U2. After eighteen months of playing together, they entered a talent show in Limerick and won the first prize of £500.

Paul McGuinness became their manager and became known as 'the fifth member of the band'. They played their first gig in London to an audience of nine people, but in 1980, their hard work was rewarded when they signed to Island Records. Their first album was called *Boy*. Their second album, *October*, did not sell as well as expected, but they kept working hard, and their third, *War*, was a huge number one hit.

U2 have recorded fourteen albums to date, all very different. They have sold over 150 million albums and are one of the most popular live bands in the world. After over forty years together, the four Dublin lads are still creating exciting new music to this day.

The three greatest U2 songs, according to American music magazine *Rolling Stone*, are 'One', 'I Still Haven't Found What I'm Looking For' and 'Beautiful Day', followed at number four by 'Sunday Bloody Sunday'.

U2 often explore political themes in their music and during their concerts. The Edge says, 'We've grown up being a political band.' Bono has been involved in humanitarian work, especially in Africa.

Other Irish bands and musicians that have made waves internationally include Van Morrison, The Cranberries, Sinead O'Connor, Thin Lizzy, Enya, Christy Moore, The Pogues, The Dubliners and Stiff Little Fingers.

Philip Treacy

HAT DESIGNER
1967

As a boy, Philip lived opposite a church. He gazed in awe at the wedding guests in their colourful hats and clothes. He never dared to dream that one day he'd be designing hats for JK Rowling and Lady Gaga!

Philip Anthony Treacy grew up in Ahascragh, a village in County Galway. He was one of eight children. His father was a baker and his mother kept hens, geese and pheasants.

At primary school, Philip asked his teacher if he could learn to sew, and from that time on he loved making things – from Christmas decorations to clothes for the doll his father bought him. His father died when he was eleven, but Philip always remembers him saying, 'Whatever makes him [Philip] happy.'

At seventeen, Philip moved to Dublin to study fashion at the National College of Art and Design. He then won a scholarship to the Royal College of Art in London. One of his hats was spotted by an influential fashion stylist, Isabella Blow, who helped kickstart his career by introducing him to famous designers.

Philip quickly became a sensation, winning many awards. In 2000, he was invited to present his own couture show during Paris Fashion Week – the first milliner* for eighty years to be given this honour.

Philip is known for his hard work and dedication. Before a big show, he often stays up all night to finish his work, listening to music to inspire him. As well as designing trailblazing hats, Philip also designed the interior of The G Hotel in Galway.

Philip has been described as 'the greatest milliner in the world'. Not bad for a boy from Galway!

*hat maker

Philip created the stylish blue hats for the French Beauxbaton Academy of Magic students who feature in *Harry Potter and the Goblet of Fire*. He has also worked as Artistic Director on musician Grace Jones's concerts.

A white Jack Russell called Mr Pig was part of Philip's family for many years. 'Mr Pig went everywhere with me,' Philip says. He brought Mr Pig to work, the cinema, fashion shows and photo shoots.

When Philip gets up in the morning, he puts his metal tailor's thimble on the middle finger of his right hand. 'My finger is now the shape of the thimble,' he says. 'My thimble is a part of me!'

'I hope I have changed the way we look at hats. They are no longer symbols of conformity but highly individual acts of rebellion.'

'I knew I had a talent. I knew I was different. Ye I understood tha talent would only get me so far, so worked hard.'

Cora Staunton

SPORTSWOMAN

1981

Cora Staunton is one of Ireland's greatest ever sportspeople. Playing Gaelic football, she has won four senior All Ireland Championships with Mayo and led her club, Carnacon, to six All Ireland titles. She has also won eleven All Star awards and is the highest-scoring forward in the history of the sport.

Cora's parents owned a farm in Castlecarra, County Mayo, and Cora and her three sisters and four brothers loved climbing trees and kicking a football around.

At seven, Cora started playing with the Ballintubber boys' team. At thirteen, she started playing for the Mayo senior team, with girls twice her age! In her first match in the Mayo jersey, she scored ten points. From then on, she was unstoppable, dedicating her life to training and matches.

When Cora's mother died, she was only sixteen. Although she found it difficult, she continued to play football.

Cora has had many physical setbacks over the years, including four broken noses, a broken collarbone and a broken jaw, but she never gave up. During one match, her nose was broken but she bandaged it up and continued to play!

In 2017, Cora became the first international player drafted to the Australian women's football league. Playing for the Greater Western Sydney Giants, she described it as a 'new adventure'. After Cora's hugely successful season with the Giants, many Irish women were invited to play Australian football, and four were signed up to teams. They called this the 'Cora effect'.

She still strives to be the best player she can be every time she steps on to a pitch. 'If you want to win you have to fight for it,' she says.

When she was a girl, Cora always wanted something sporty for Christmas – a dartboard, a bike or a new football. She hated dresses, and wore a trouser suit for her confirmation.

As well as football, Cora played basketball, handball and soccer at school. She also showed talent as a rugby player. Cora's own sporting heroes include Sonia O'Sullivan and Roy Keane.

Cora has a master's degree in Health Promotion and works with the Mayo Travellers Support Group, a role she finds hugely rewarding.

Dreamers of Tomorrow

Katie Mullan
INTERNATIONAL HOCKEY PLAYER
Katie began playing hockey at school. Strong, fast and a gifted leader, she was captain of the Irish team who won a silver medal at the 2018 Women's Hockey World Cup. She has a master's in Biomedical Engineering and, as well as playing for the Irish team, plays professional hockey in Germany.

James Whelton
ENTREPRENEUR
James set up the not-for-profit organisation Coder Dojo when he was eighteen, along with Bill Liao, to teach children how to code. Within a year there were Coder Dojos all over the world. Now operating in over ninety countries, its one rule is 'Above all, be cool.'

Joanne O'Riordan
JOURNALIST
A keen writer from an early age, Joanne is a sports journalist for the *Irish Times*. One of only seven people in the world with Tetra-amelia Syndrome, which means she has no limbs, Joanne has never let it stop her. She has given TEDx talks and a speech at the United Nations.

Emma Dabiri
WRITER AND BROADCASTER
Interested in history and injustice from a young age, instead of making her First Communion, Emma wrote and produced an anti-slavery treatise. She has a PhD in Sociology and teaches at university level. She has also presented television programmes and written a book called *Don't Touch My Hair*.

Dr Sindy Joyce
ACADEMIC AND HUMAN RIGHTS ACTIVIST

Sindy is the first Traveller – or Mincéir in her own language, Cant – to graduate with a PhD. For her doctorate, she interviewed young Travellers about their experiences of urban spaces. In 2019, President Michael D Higgins appointed Sindy to his panel of special advisors, the Council of State.

Aiden Harris Igiehon
ATHLETE

Aidan started playing basketball at twelve with the Dublin Lions. In 2014 he won a high school basketball scholarship and moved to New York. Now considered one of the top college players in the US, he hopes to play for the NBA in the future. At six foot ten inches, his nickname is 'Irish Hulk'.

Adam Harris
SOCIAL ENTREPRENEUR

Adam is the Founder-CEO of AsIAm, an organisation working to build an Ireland where every person with autism can 'live and succeed as they are'. Diagnosed with Asperger's syndrome when he was five, his own experiences inspired him to set up AsIAm while still studying for his Leaving Certificate.

Hozier
MUSICIAN

Andrew Hozier-Byrne loved music from a young age and began writing songs at fifteen. He sang with choral group Anúna before releasing his own EP, 'Take Me to Church', in 2013. He is now winning awards and captivating music lovers all over the world.

ABOUT THE AUTHOR

Sarah Webb writes for all ages, from young children to adults. *A Sailor Went to Sea, Sea, Sea: Favourite Rhymes from an Irish Childhood* (with Steve McCarthy) won the Irish Book Awards Children's Book of the Year (Junior) in 2017, and *Blazing a Trail: Irish Women Who Changed the World* (with Lauren O'Neill) won the Irish Book Awards Children's Book of the Year (Senior) in 2018.

Sarah also runs writing clubs and programmes children's events for several Irish book festivals. www.sarahwebb.ie

ABOUT THE ILLUSTRATOR

Graham Corcoran is an illustrator from Dublin. His work can be seen in magazines, exhibitions, book covers and advertising campaigns around the world. Graham has also designed several animated children's television series for RTÉ, BBC and Nick Jr. *Dare to Dream* is his first illustrated book for children. www.grahamcorcoran.com

First published 2019 by
The O'Brien Press Ltd.
12 Terenure Road East,
Rathgar, Dublin 6, D06 HD27, Ireland.
Tel: +353 1 4923333; Fax: +353 1 4922777
E-mail: books@obrien.ie; Website: www.obrien.ie
Reprinted 2019.
The O'Brien Press is a member of Publishing Ireland.

ISBN: 978-1-78849-127-3

10 9 8 7 6 5 4 3 2
24 23 22 21 20 19

Printed by EDELVIVES, Spain.
The paper in this book is produced using pulp from managed forests.

Published in:

DUBLIN
UNESCO
City of Literature

Acknowledgements

Sarah: A huge thanks to the whole team at The O'Brien Press for their help and support, most especially my editor Eoin O'Brien, who added his own touch of magic to this book, designer Emma Byrne and illustrator Graham Corcoran for his gloriously colourful art work.

I'd also like to sincerely thank Marian Keyes and Nigel Curtin from dlr Libraries. I would not have been able to undertake the research for this book without the support of the library service. Nigel went out of his way to find me books, articles and pamphlets, and I'm very grateful for his knowledge and assistance.

Dr Abigail Ruth Freeman from Science Foundation Ireland was incredibly helpful, and many of the modern scientists she suggested appear in this book.

Martina Devlin kindly read many of the entries and gave me invaluable feedback.

And thanks also to: Mary Hannigan, Shane Hegarty, Justine Kyle McGrath, Professor Susan McKenna-Lawlor and Dr Ruth Barton for all their help with the research, and to Doireann Ní Ghríofa for use of an extract from her poem 'Maude, Enthralled'.

Graham: I'd like to thank Sarah Webb for inviting me along on this amazing journey and giving me the opportunity to illustrate such an inspiring array of talented men and women from Irish history. Thank you to everyone at The O'Brien Press, especially Emma Byrne for being an enormous help throughout the process.